Carmen Sylva, Mary A.. trl Mitchell

A heart regained

a novel

Carmen Sylva, Mary A.. trl Mitchell

A heart regained
a novel

ISBN/EAN: 9783741148989

Manufactured in Europe, USA, Canada, Australia, Japa

Cover: Foto ©Thomas Meinert / pixelio.de

Manufactured and distributed by brebook publishing software
(www.brebook.com)

Carmen Sylva, Mary A.. trl Mitchell

A heart regained

A HEART REGAINED.

A HEART REGAINED

A Novel

By CARMEN SYLVA

Translated by

MRS. MARY A. MITCHELL

BOSTON

CUPPLES AND HURD

1888

CONTENTS.

A HEART REGAINED.

CHAPTER I.

A STORMY NIGHT.

THE tear-laden, budding branches seemed to writhe with pain as the spring storm bent and blew them wildly against the window. The thunder and lightning had disappeared; but not so the black clouds, which continued to pour down their watery contents, making the night still darker.

From comparison, the cosey library, with its soft study-lamp and sweet-scented bouquet of lily-of-the-valley, seemed all the quieter.

In the light of this lamp sits a girlish

figure at the writing-table, on which she
rests both arms, while her eyes are
buried in a letter. Her slender fingers
stroke away the auburn hair which lies
in waves on her temples and is fastened
in a bright golden curl low on her neck.
Her forehead is broad, almost angular;
her nose delicate, a little too short, or
perhaps it is the shadow of her hand
which has the effect of shortening it.

Her hand denotes the same firmness
as the broad forehead, and gives the
impression that it is accustomed to hold
fast the reins of government, and to
subdue rebellious spirits.

What can that letter contain? She
has read and reread it so often for the
last hour that she must surely know
every line by heart.

"Most Gracious Lady, — It may be a thank-
less service which I am about to render, and yet
I cannot refrain. I can no longer see you betrayed,

" Your husband has long ceased to love you,
and his illicit connection has given him that which
an unjust Heaven has denied you, — a son !

" You must have wondered that I should have
left your service, where I enjoyed all that heart
could desire, or ambition covet. I could no longer
be a witness of what I knew. Forgive my opening
your eyes. At least, now you are warned, and
know what to do.

" Should you need me, I am always at your
service.

" PHILLIPINE REISIG."

The window shook, the climbing ivy
beat against the pane ; the chimney
moaned with a minor strain of woe.

Leonie was deaf to all ; and, but for
the trembling hand which sought to
keep the hot blood from mounting
to her temples, she might have seemed
a marble statue.

There was a time when her only
answer to a question of Burkhard's truth
would have been to throw herself into

his beloved arms, for she loved him
with all the passion of natures which
accompany golden hair and gray eyes.

She now pressed her hand to her
mouth, to which the tightly pressed
upper lip gave a certain severity, and
which then supported her full chin, as
thought after thought threw shadows
on eye and brow.

Had the letter been anonymous, she
would have thrown it in the fire without deigning it a second look ; but the
writer seemed ready to prove what she
asserted.

" Phillipine Reisig." Leonie had been
tempted to feel jealous of her husband's
partiality for " Pinchen ; " and when the
latter left her service, she fancied that it
was to hide her pretty face from Burkhard. How could any one help loving
him, with his deep blue eyes, his distinguished figure, his flowing brown hair

and beard, his sweet smile and sonorous voice? How could all this be withstood?

But alas! alas! The day came when Leonie saw those eyes grow cold, and heard that voice sound harsh and utter words of reproach, because she had no child. At this remembrance, a shudder passed through her girlish frame.

" His illicit love has given him what an unjust Heaven has refused you, — a son." Here was the sentence which held Leonie's eye like a magnet; and it seemed as if she could have borne his infidelity, had not this scoffing fate been the cause of it.

" Now you are warned, and not un-armed." She almost laughed at the word. " Unarmed," — so completely un-armed; the unhappy wife face to face with the still more unhappy mother, bound hand and foot. She did not hate her rival as much as she hated herself.

"Consider what to do." Yes, that she would, coolly and dispassionately, as though it did not concern her. Hence she sat this stormy night, "considering what to do," but she could not decide. In the luxuriously furnished room near by, Burkhard was asleep. He slept quietly and soundly, for he had been up since three the previous morning, shooting the last of the woodcock.

"Consider what to do." Be silent. Was it, then, all over between them? The sweet ties all broken, — the deep, complete confidence uprooted? She could do nothing for that woman. The child was a bastard, and could never be the heir.

"O Burkhard, Burkhard!" she murmured. "Have I not made you happy, and is this the reason that you are false? I have thought of you day and night." She then examined scrupulously in what

she should have been other than she
was. Perchance she had not been affec-
tionate, but it was not natural for her to
be demonstrative.

Her love had something of a volcanic
nature, but its warmth was chilled by
her childlessness; for motherhood is the
true woman's passion, before which love
itself pales if not a minister to it. Leonie
turned away, hungry in heart, from her
beautiful palace and vast demesne, envy-
ing the poorest woman who cared for
her six little ones, while expecting the
seventh. Yes, her eyes looked longingly
on the very hound that lay in the midst
of her barking, playful sucklings. She
loved children, and all children loved
her.

Perhaps her husband did not find her
pretty. He was so handsome, perhaps
nature had taken a revenge in disap-
pointing him in his standard of womanly

beauty; and yet he used to praise her
hair, her hands and teeth and classically
formed feet. He had once found much
to admire; but that time was passed,
and she had not observed the change,
for vanity and jealousy had no part in
her. Thus thought after thought racked
the poor, sore heart, as the wind the
groaning trees and trembling leaves.

Then her eye fell on the words " son "
and " what to do; " and the quieting
response, " Nothing, do nothing."
seemed to sound in her ear. " Is he
not sufficiently punished in the future
of his child? I shall be silent. Oh, of
what can I speak to him? How could I
mention the subject to him? and to what
use? For the future I shall commune
with my books; they, at least, lie only
through ignorance. I shall be silent!"

As she came to this decision, she
heard a knock at the door; a quick,

loud knock, which frightened her.
What could a knock at her door at that
hour mean? Had the outer gates been
left unlocked? who could have stolen
in? Her heart seemed to stand still a
moment; then it occurred to her, that
perhaps Pinchen had come to add to the
tale, which perhaps, after all, was the
imagining of her jealousy; and, taking
the lamp, she walked quickly to the
door, which she opened, throwing the
light of the lamp abroad. Seeing noth·
ing, she determined to go out; but her
foot tripped on something lying on the
ground. Looking down she perceived
an exquisitely beautiful child, with golden
hair, and blue eyes turned on her like
a ray of heavenly peace.

Quickly she knelt over the baby, and,
placing the lamp aside, ejaculated "My
God!"

A cold hand was laid on her shoulder; and, looking up, she saw a tall, gaunt figure, whose glittering eyes gazed at her with an indescribable anguish, and whose long dishevelled hair gave it a ghostly aspect.

"Where is he?" whispered the dry, bleached lips, — "where? This is his house, but I cannot find him."

"Whom do you seek?" inquired Leonie in her deep contralto voice, as she arose and examined the woman, than whom she was a whole head taller, and whose thin hands wrung each other with the agony of despair, while the muscles of her face worked convulsively.

"Good God! good God!" whispered the poor creature hoarsely. "Who are you, and where is Burkhard? Do you call him so? or has he deceived me in his name too, in order that I might not find him?"

Leonie stared at the unhappy victim,

and then at the child, while she said slowly, "Burkhard is my husband's name."

At these words, the stranger started as if she had seen an apparition, and staggering back she leaned against the wall for support, and screamed, "No, no, not his wife! He had no wife, Burkhard had no wife."

A tempest of outraged feeling and sadness swept over Leonie's expressive countenance; but heavenly compassion conquered as she asked gently, "Is this his child? come with me," and she raised up the baby, and returned to her room.

Turning towards the woman, she perceived her sinking to a low ottoman, with the blood pouring from her lips. Quickly Leonie laid the child down, and went to the woman's side, placed all the cushions within reach beneath her, and opened wide the window in order to give her air.

The poor invalid whispered, "He came no more to me, he came no more to me, when I showed him the child, because he feared that he must marry me, — his Mary, — his love; and I sickened, and now I must die. The whole day long have I sought him. I must find him. I hid in the garden, and stole into the house when all was quiet, but he did not come out; and when I saw the light here I thought, 'He is there, thinking of me,' and I came — and find — and find his wife." She beat her breast wildly, and struggling for breath continued, "Have pity on the child! Oh, not in the orphan-house, my child! not in cruel hands, my child! It was not his fault that he was born. I thought that he would be my angel, my guardian angel, who would redeem my honor. My beautiful boy! And now I find the wife!" She rocked from side to side, and dark shadows crept over her eyes and brows.

Leonie had never looked on death, but she felt that this must be it, and she trembled in every limb.

The room had grown cold, and the child stirred. The woman raised herself, and murmured "My baby." Leonie brought it to her, and wrapped a shawl around her.

The little one crept up to his mother, and tried to open her dress in order to reach her breast; but in a feeble voice she said, "Not a drop, Baldo, not a drop! My poor boy is so hungry!"

"I can help him," cried Leonie, in self-forgetting ardor. She was in the habit of keeping her spirit-lamp by her, in order to make a cup of tea when she wrote late at night. Soon it was lighted;

milk was warmed and sweetened, and greedily drank by the child. The mother raised her wondering eyes, and saying, " Be a mother," laid her head back, and drew a long, labored breath. Her eyes were cast upwards, her lips parted, and the heart stood still.

Leonie was not proof against the awe which the first sight of death brings with it, but she had a strong soul. She closed the staring eyes; and, finding that she could not close the mouth, she placed a pillow behind the head, so that the chin rested on the breast, and thus pressed the lips together.

The infant instinctively sought the maternal breast, but, finding it cold and rigid, pursed up its rosy lips in fright, and began to cry. Leonie lifted the little one, and commenced to sing to it the beautiful hymn, " In the midst of life we are in death." Like the tones of an organ, the rich contralto voice was heard above the outside storm, while the young woman walked slowly up and down before the dead; her little burden finally closed its wondering eyes in sweet sleep, as if abandoning an enigma beyond its comprehension. Then she wrapped it in a soft white shawl, and laid it gently on the divan, and seated herself to consider what was next to be done.

Revenge was within her grasp. She had only to awaken Burkhard, to witness him suffer in a second the punishment of years of sin.

All the long hours of agony which she had borne seized and tore her heart; and as she pressed her fingers to her eyes, they seemed on fire. She sprang to her feet; and as her eyes fell on the dead and on the sleeper, an inexpressible tenderness drew her to the little being who at that moment smiled in its dreams.

It was the child of the only man whom she had ever loved, and whom she still loved more than herself. Would she take revenge on him through the dread spectacle which here made her own blood run cold? No, no! he must be prepared for it.

Not wishing to leave the child alone, she raised it in her arms, and, lighted by the night-lamp, placed it in her own bed. She then seated herself on the edge of her husband's bed, and called him. He awoke, and, surprised at seeing her still dressed, inquired, " Has any thing happened?"

" Much has happened to-night," she answered wearily, as she handed him the letter, and drew forward a light, first shading the child with the curtain.

The veins on Burkhard's forehead swelled as he said, " And you believe this?"

She put back the curtain, and let the light fall on the sleeper.

" Baldo ! " he cried. The baby awoke, stretched out its little hands, and lisped, " Papa."

" Kiss our son," said Leonie.

" Leonie, you can — you will " —

" I can and I will. So help me, God ! "

The inner struggle was visible in the workings of her brow, and her weariness of soul made her look like the Fate who has just cut the thread of destiny ; but she calmly waited until he had regained sufficient control to say, " How did you find it ? "

" I did not find it. She found me."

" You ! *She* found you ! But she knew neither my name nor my residence, nor — nor " —

" Nor that you had a wife. No, she sought you in order to die beside you."

" To die! Do you speak of Mary ? "

" She said that was her name."

" But why do you say she wished to die ? "

" Oh, no ! she did not *wish* to die. She did not wish to leave her child ; but she lies dead there in my room."

These words fell like drops of molten lead. Burkhard held his left hand before his eyes. With the right, which his wife still held, he clung to her with the grasp of a drowning man. By it she measured his agony, and his love for the deceased ; but she did not move, and after a few minutes said, " Do not think that she was a suicide. She died in my arms, from a hemorrhage."

His teeth chattered, and his powerful frame trembled.

Leonie longed to say something to help him in his suffering, but her own agony was too great. After a long pause she asked, "Will you not look at her? She is very beautiful."

"Papa," lisped the baby, and again slept.

Burkhard looked at the child, and said, "Leonie, you are my anchor and my salvation. But for thee, I would go mad." He raised her hand to his lips; he then rose, and, staggering towards the library-door, looked back inquiringly.

Leonie merely said, "In my room. The lamp is burning. I shall remain here."

He groped through the hall, towards a door from which a faint light came. For a moment he could not decide to enter, and then staggered forward, and fell upon his knees by the corpse.

The storm had renewed its fury, and broke a tree which struck the window as it fell to the ground. The chimney seemed filled with the howling of uncanny spirits. Burkhard remained a long while, then returned to the sleep-ing-room, pale and worn, and afraid to look his wife in the eye. She, however, had lain down, burying her face in the little one's curls, and now feigned sleep in order to spare him. He went down stairs stealthily, and paced his study floor until day dawned.

Leonie's heart had beaten until she heard each pulsation, while Burkhard tarried by the dead woman. When he again opened her door, it seemed to stand still; and when she ceased to hear his footstep, — that step for which she had ever listened with all the ardor of a bride, — it seemed to her as if she had lost him forever. Farther and farther it died away in the silent house; and she buried her face in the pillow, and wept bitterly.

Her tears seemed to loosen the gnaw·

ing grief which had benumbed her soul ;
but then came a helpless, hopeless feeling, as if time had come to an end, and
the sun were dimmed forever. She
reproached herself with having left him
so long alone this awful night. But
was he not there heart and soul with the
dead? Would she not have disturbed
him? "All is past! All is gone! Dear
God, help me not to murmur!" She,
the strong-willed, the unbending, felt
herself as weak as a little child. She
raised herself up, and, pushing the hair
from her forehead, exclaimed, "How
can I be so weak and cowardly?" Her
glance fell on the little one whom she
had almost forgotten ; and she said to
herself, "Poor little fellow! will he say
'mother,' that I may hear the blessed
word for which I have so longed, —
'mother'! Perhaps 'mamma' will be
more easily learned, but 'mother'

expresses more. Dare I? How can I
deserve that which I have not conceived,
or for which I have not labored? Oh,
yes, I dare, I dare. My life is shattered, my heart's blood is wept out, my
happiness gone; nothing more remains
for me. Mother, mother!" and again
and again she kissed the little feet and
limbs, which she had bared, repeating,
as she wept, "How pretty! how
pretty!"

The day broke; and Leonie realized
that she must do something to prevent
the maid, who would soon come to dust
her room, being frightened and raising
an alarm. She went quickly into the
dressing-room, which was separated from
the bedroom by a *portière*, combed her
thick hair, and, fastening it on the top
of her head, sprang into the bath, which
cooled her burning face and refreshed
her weary limbs. She leaned back and

smiled as it occurred to her that she must use a tub to wash the baby, because she did not possess a child's bath ; and how warm ought the water to be, and whether he would kick. She determined to lose no time in procuring the best medical books on the care of children.

But while busy with such thoughts, she heard, notwithstanding the splashing of the water and the drizzling rain, a little voice. She jumped out of the bath, wrapped a sheet around her, and hastened to the bed where the little one lay as rosy as a shrimp, and looking at her with great staring eyes. As he felt her soft face close to his neck, he buried his fingers in her hair, laughing and crowing.

The play would have continued much longer, had not Leonie heard sounds of moving about down-stairs. She put on a white cashmere morning-dress, and rang for her maid, to whom she said with a beaming countenance, "See, Melanie, what the good God has sent me, — an angel. A poor woman came to my door last night, and, as it was raining hard, I brought her in ; and she lies dead in my room! I do not know who she is ; but she bequeathed me the child, and said his name was Baldo. Give orders to have a bier brought immediately, and the poor woman taken to the hall in the garden ; and then warm some milk for my child." It was out! She had said "my child," and it had not burned her lips. Good God! "My child!" Surely a birth had been that night, and she rejoiced.

She began again to wonder if he could drink or creep, and once more rolled him on the pillow in order to make him crow. Her woman's thoughts then busied themselves with the question of what he should wear; he then had on only a little shirt, and she thought it would be a pity to hide such loveliness; but Melanie would know. The latter, however, was not thinking of the child, but had called together the whole household, and was holding forth with as much authority as if she had been an eyewitness of all that had happened.

Burkhard heard all the noise in the house, the steady step pass by his room as though something heavy were being carried, the subdued whispering; but he had not the courage to open his door, or even to ring. He busied himself with his toilet, which was always a matter of much care to him. To-day all his movements were slow, as those of one grown suddenly old. The weather was not sufficiently cold to cool his burning brow, or to soothe his throbbing temples; the perfumed water which he always sprinkled on his long beard had grown offensive.

He threw himself into a chair, and filed and polished his nails, while his pride sought grounds on which to blame his wife. Leonie had crushed him. She had in cold blood driven a sword through his heart, and had not even stretched forth a hand to stanch the fatal wound. She had no heart, that he had long known. That other one had loved him and died for him.

All the spirits of evil seemed alive in his soul. Hate, suspicion, bitterness, drove him hither and thither unmercifully, like a withered leaf.

This modern Orestes knew no oracle, no temple whence to seek relief; and all his proud spirit and deep learning were unable to drive the Furies from their stronghold. But to the modern as to the ancient came relief in female guise.

Burkhard's door was opened; and in the bright sunlight there appeared a vision of that for which he had wished and prayed, but on which he had learned to look as unattainable.

Leonie, in her white robe, and crowned with the halo of her golden hair, stood holding his child with its father's eyes. Before he had time to rise, it lay in his lap, and she knelt before him, teaching it to play with his watch-chain, and to "listen to papa's tic-tac," saying, "Is he not beautiful, Burkhard? Only look at his little cheek! and when he stretches his arm, there is a lovely dimple in his elbow, and four more in his tiny knuckles. You must see him take his bath to-night. We could not have it this morning, for we were too hungry. A little bed must be purchased, and placed near mine. No one must feed him but myself. O good Heaven, look at him, he is so pretty!—

Baldo, tic-tac. — Now he wants the scissors. How can one refuse a child something without making it cry? "

She chatted on in this way for some time, while faint smiles passed over Burkhard's countenance ; but he only dared to look at her once. She did not appear to notice this, — only the child. When he bent his mouth towards the little fellow, and blew aside its curls, as if ashamed to show it any affection in the presence of Leonie, she exclaimed, " Oh, that is not the way to kiss him ! So, and so, and so ; " and she held up each little limb to Burkhard. The little one laughed as his father's beard tickled him.

Leonie, hearing the hearse and the men's steps on the gravel, spoke all the faster of the child. Just as they were carrying out the coffin, Burkhard turned his head to the window, and became as white as death.

"Every thing has been arranged," said Leonie. "Not a suspicion rests on you."

He must drink the cup of mortification to the dregs. She uttered no word of reproach ; on the contrary, she was only anxious to shield and help him. Her very silence was evidence of the chasm that lay between them.

Were it not for the child, life would be unendurable. Unless when speaking to or of him, a gloomy silence prevailed. If Burkhard chanced to say that he was going out, she never asked when he would return. Should he return unexpectedly, she did not run to meet him, for she remembered how she used to do it in happy days. It was all so hard, — so hard ! Nothing, save the care of the baby, was done spontaneously.

Burkhard felt his heart full of tenderness for his wife, but a certain shyness prevented his showing it. She, believing herself disagreeable to him, studiously tried to appear cold. The sounding-board of their love was broken, and could give forth no more harmony. How soft soever the hand that struck the chord, the note sounded false. The unspoken something continually wove a thick veil between them, through which each word or look was distorted.

CHAPTER II.

BALDO.

"BURKHARD! Burkhard! come, come quickly! He is standing alone, and has taken a step."

It was Leonie who thus called, as she rushed down-stairs into her husband's room, which he occupied now alone, because a child disturbed him; and she desired to be a true mother, since Heaven had granted her the privilege, — indeed, had imposed it on her.

She was very much excited by so young a child's having taken a step, and Burkhard had hastened up-stairs to see the wonder; but she had marvelled that he did not sympathize with her feeling. Surely the key to his heart was gradually slipping from her grasp, and her passionate devotion had made her slow to observe it.

She had imagined that he would be perfectly happy, now that his great desire was fulfilled; and she flattered herself that she had been in a measure instrumental in procuring him that happiness.

But he could not be cheerful. The child was a continual reproach to him. He fancied that were it not for him, whose resemblance to his mother increased every day, it would have been easier to forget Mary and that dreadful night. Furthermore, he was jealous of Leonie's tenderness for the boy, which she showed with all the earnestness of her nature. "She has never loved me," he said a hundred times to himself; and the thought lent a quiver to the lip, and a sadness to the eye, which made Leonie believe that he still mourned for the dead, and impatiently she would soliloquize, " There remains to him what was best of her : she was only a servant." When perhaps he most longed for her caresses, they were withheld on account of that eternal shadow which was far from his thoughts.

He remembered Leonie's young love, and her touching resignation that she had not children, which sometimes brought him near confessing his own faithlessness. But now she seemed haughty in his eyes. She appeared to tolerate him merely for the sake of the boy, of whom she was as proud as though she had borne him.

Still Leonie wondered over her idol's precocity in saying " mamma," " ta," and " bath." The latter he applied to every stream and river. He was very quick in attempting new words and in walking; and she was untiring in teaching him, unconscious of the danger of over-exciting the young brain. When only a year and a half old, he spoke a good deal, and his voice seemed to fill the whole house.

Burkhard was conscious that there was much conjecturing rife, and that not a few recognized the father's eyes in the boy. Leonie's perfect happiness made her blind and deaf to it all. "O Burkhard!" she would say, "who could have thought that our lives would have been so happy? Now nothing more is wanting." It was on his lips to say, "I want you," but, feeling that he had no right to the reproach, he was silent; and his silence estranged them, for in her heart she accused him of ingratitude.

The child became the idol of the house; he seemed the pivot on which every thing turned, so that soon aught else, even guests, were a disturbance. Baldo was not spoiled: he was one of those characters that have ever even more love to give than they can receive.

One day the following conversation took place : —

"And so you found me in a flower, mamma. Which flower? Show it to me."

"It is now faded, darling."

"And an angel left me there. Where did he bring me from?"

"Probably from heaven. You were too little to tell me where you came from."

"Why did you not ask the angel?"

"I saw his wings only, just as he was flying back to heaven."

"And were you sure that I was for you?"

"Oh, yes! quite sure. You were in my garden."

"And was papa glad?"

The quick blood flew to Leonie's face as she answered, —

"Oh, so glad! For we had prayed to God every day to send us a baby."

Burkhard had listened to this prattle while apparently buried in his newspaper by the fire.

Leonie sat working quietly at her spinning-wheel; but at the last word the thread broke, and she stooped down to fasten it with her small silver hook. And the boy continued, —

"Then we must pray to him to send me a little brother or sister."

The husband and wife exchanged glances; and Leonie said gently, with a sigh, "Have you not yet enough? You have your goat-carriage, your pony, your big dog and little puppy; and you are not contented."

The child seemed lost in thought, and his eyes grew deeper as he answered,

"Yes, I have enough. If I could only divide it, it would be nicer."

From that day forward she always took him with her to visit the poor, and encouraged him to give of his own clothes and playthings. Soon he was looked upon as a messenger from heaven, as he appeared with his golden hair and soft voice. The latter was clear as a bell; and when Leonie's contralto accompanied him, Burkhard used to call it his evening concert. As he rode out with his father, his locks flying in the wind, the people came to their doors to admire the picture,—the handsome, respected man, and the graceful boy, followed by a pair of beautiful hounds.

Leonie would leave the teaching of her child to no one. She charged herself with the duty, and was astonished at his cleverness. Every thing seemed so easy to him, that she was tempted to

urge him further than was prudent for
a boy scarcely six years old. She determined to have him examined by two
prominent teachers, for she feared that
she did not advance him sufficiently.
They were very much astonished at his
answers, but advised her not to require
too much, warning her of the danger
of over-exciting his brain. She looked
at them in astonishment. He should
have all her strength of mind; and so
he had to a certain point, but here
seemed to enter the ethereal which perchance the departing spirit of the dead
mother bequeathed him, — a something
which made people say as they looked
at Leonie and Baldo, " It is easy to see
he is not of her blood, else would he be
more robust."

Burkhard had lately taken refuge from
his own thoughts in a public-spirited
activity. He established a savings bank,

a cattle-market. He purchased the most improved agricultural machines, and lent them to the peasants. The people with one voice proclaimed him their universal benefactor. Through his influence a railway was built, an exhibition was held, the breeding of cattle and the management of crops were better understood in the neighborhood.

An orphan-asylum and a deaf-and-dumb institution owed their existence to him. Happiness and success followed his footsteps, so that he was almost an object of envy. His winning, persuasive manner led men to believe that they were carrying out their own convictions in following his suggestions.

At first all this energy was powerless to win him a loving look as of old from Leonie; but by degrees she became proud of him as she heard on all sides of his noble deeds.

The "harvest-home" came, and Baldo
was the leader of the children in happy
sports. Then the "threshing" with its
accompanying dancing and singing.
Altogether, such a happy state of things
existed on the estate as could be found
only under the best of landlords.

The surrounding gentry came to the
festivities, and began to find Leonie quite
agreeable, notwithstanding that her un-
usual cleverness had heretofore held them
In awe.

Often parents of unmanageable children begged her permission to bring
them to her. At first she hesitated, lest
they might spoil Baldo, whom she gov-
erned by love; but discovering that he
was benefited, and his emulation strengthened, by companionship, it ended by her
having quite a school of his little play-
mates.

Baldo, like a guardian spirit, had

awakened all that was best and noblest in both parents. The children called him " Friedlein " ' because of the peculiar power which he possessed of making peace in all their quarrels, and of saving them from punishment. The people loved to relate how he had received a blow which was meant for another, and looked up at the angry peasant with such a heavenly expression, that the latter threw away his whip, convinced that he had met an angel. The boy whom he had in this instance saved became henceforth his inseparable shadow, so that one commonly heard the remark, " There go Friedlein and his Toni." They built log houses together, roofing them with bark and moss, and provisioning them with red apples, where they played keeping house.

There was only one person in the

' Little peace.

neighborhood to whom Baldo showed a
dislike, and, strange to say, he was alone
in this feeling; on the contrary, the ob-
object of his prejudice was commonly
known as " the pretty Wilma," and it
was only her want of fortune which prevented her having many suitors. Her
figure was tall and willowy; she wore
her rich brown hair short, leaving her
white neck and forehead entirely uncov-
ered, with the exception of the left temple over which a curl fell. Her well-
arched eyebrows shaded hazel eyes that
were in turn brilliant and languid. Her
skin was snow-white, her cheek a delicate changing pink; and when the short
lips parted, they showed dazzling rows
of teeth.

On foot or on horseback, in hunting
or fishing parties, in dancing or target-
shooting, Wilma was always foremost in
life and spirit, and the object of much

contention among her admirers. Indeed, it was hinted that she was respon-
sible for two duels and one suicide ; but
that was only gossip born of jealousy of
the pretty Wilma, who spoiled so many
girls' love affairs, appropriating the admirers, while she herself remained as
unmoved as a marble statue.

Leonie had seen this beauty but seldom, for her many occupations prevented
her taking an interest in the gatherings
where Wilma shone ; which made her
often the subject of the latter's sarcasm.
This was also unknown to its victim, for
she was not one to whom gossip-carriers
were apt to come ; not even Burkhard,
who, since that eventful night, could not
divest himself of a certain awe for her
strong, noble character.

"Mother," said Baldo one day, — he
always addressed her as " mother "
when he had any thing of importance

to communicate, — "she called me Friedlein; and I am not Friedlein to her, only to those whom I love; and I hate her."

"Of whom are you speaking, child? and how can you utter so naughty a word? You cannot be called Friedlein if you hate any one."

"Why, you know, mother, she whom papa finds pretty, and who rides with us sometimes, and who speaks so fast, and such stupid things of which she knows nothing. She speaks of wicked things, mother, which Toni would never mention."

Leonie became suddenly serious, and for a moment seemed not to quite understand the boy, but looked as if a spectre appeared in the distance; and with an effort at self-control, she said, "When my Friedlein hears people say wicked things, he must say to himself that perhaps they never had a careful mother."

"And when I see them turn their back on the poor, mother, what must I do?"

"Then Friedlein must go very quietly, when no one sees, and help the poor. One must be very good in order to deserve so pretty a name."

"But when *she* calls me so, mother" —

"Can you not bear it, child, on account of so many good people who gave you the name? Who knows but some time you may be able to do her a little good?" sighed Leonie.

After this conversation with his mother, Baldo said to Toni, in their playhouse. "Do you know, when Wilma falls, and breaks her leg, we will carry her in here, and take care of her."

"But how shall we manage to have her break her leg?" asked Toni.

" Oh, we will ask God."

" No, Friedlein, we will make a hole into which the horse will step."

" Oh, no, Toni ! Then that would be our work and not God's."

" Well, what shall we lay her on ? "

" On moss."

" On nettles," suggested the revengeful Toni, to whom Wilma had been rough when he did not get out of her way; of which, indeed, he was purposely guilty, because his Friedlein hated her, and because she was so haughty towards the friend whom he followed like a dog who snarls and bites the hand lifted against his protector.

" She whom papa finds so pretty," fell from the child's innocent lips on poor Leonie's sore heart like a lump of ice that would not melt. " She whom papa finds pretty." · She was provoked with herself, that these words should make

such an impression ; but with her newly-
learned reserve towards Burkhard, she
determined to be silent and to observe.
She saw that Wilma was constantly occupied about her husband, and, uncon-
sciously to him, was entrapping him in
her wiles, while he certainly was not indifferent to her charms.

With her accustomed self-control, however, she showed neither irritation nor
bitterness, but turned with still more in-
tense love to the child. She did not like
to see Burkhard and Wilma take Baldo
with them on their rides, and had suc-
ceeded more than once in preventing it.
But one day the child pleaded so earnestly, impatiently insisting that nothing
could happen to him, he had grown such
a big boy, she unwillingly gave her permission. During their absence she wandered aimlessly through the house, took
up a book, and read and reread it until
the twilight began to fall,

The servants had set the table on the terrace for supper, and still there was no sound of horses' feet. Leonie grew very uneasy, and walked up and down on the gravel walk which led to the gate. Had she but known in what direction they had gone, she would have driven to meet them. She reproached herself for not having accompanied them; for who could tell what foolishness that madcap Wilma might be guilty of, not considering how much a little child could bear? In imagination she saw Baldo carried home senseless, and Burkhard with broken limbs, until the perspiration from anxiety stood on her forehead, just as she recognized the sound of horses in the distance, and father and son soon dismounted.

Heretofore Baldo was always the first to jump from the saddle, and spring into his mother's arms; but to-day he waited to be lifted down.

"What is the matter, my child? and why are you so late?" asked Leonie.

"A thousand pardons, Leonie," answered Burkhard. "We rode rather far, and Baldo became suddenly so tired that we had to go slowly; hence our late return."

She drew the boy towards the lamp, and said, "How pale you look! Has any thing happened?"

"I am only tired; it was so hot."

"But it is now nice and cool," suggested Burkhard.

"Yes, it is cold — no, hot," added the child wearily, as he stared about him vacantly.

Leonie looked reproachfully at her husband; and taking Baldo in her arms she carried him up stairs without a word, undressed him, put him to bed, and brought him some bread and milk.

He tasted the milk, but refused the

bread; said he was too tired to eat, and wished to go to sleep. In a few minutes his deep breathing showed that he was in a heavy sleep.

Leonie called the nurse, and told her to remain by the bed until she returned.

Down stairs she found her husband impatient at her delay; he was hungry, but would not commence alone to eat. He scolded her for being so uneasy concerning the boy, and said that it would be much better that he should go to school where he would not be pampered. She said nothing. Her heart was too full of care and anxiety to argue while her husband was so irritated.

The dew began to fall, the evening became cooler, and they went into the drawing-room, discontented with themselves and with each other. Leonie went up-stairs once, and finding the boy still pale, but sleeping, she came down

again, and took up a book; while Burkhard also read, and smoked. A moth
flew between them, burned itself at the
lamp, and fell dead on the tablecloth.
Leonie looked at it, and wondered why
so many would persistently fly into the
flame that had already burned thousands.
Her glance wandered to Burkhard; and
it seemed on the tip of her tongue to
warn him, and by a tender look to draw
him back to her before it was too late.
She was on the point of rising, drawing
a stool to his side, and opening her heart,
when some one knocked carefully at
the door.

Burkhard called out "Come in;" and
the nurse entered, saying, "I don't
know what is the matter with the child.
He cries out in his sleep, his cheeks are
very red, and he rubs his head continually, and I cannot waken him."

Leonie did not wait to hear the last

word, but flew up-stairs, and threw herself on her knees by the bed. Baldo's face was purple. He opened his eyes, looked at her, and cried out, "Oh, my head! my head!"

She called for some ice, and ordered the carriage to be sent immediately for the doctor. She put warm cloths to his feet, and ice to his head, which seemed to relieve him; at least, he opened his eyes, and said "good mamma," and again fell asleep, but soon resumed calling out loud.

When the physician came, she did not dare question him. He approved of all that she had done, and ordered compresses to be applied to his body; but he looked so serious, she felt almost paralyzed.

Burkhard asked many questions, and groaned aloud as the doctor pronounced the words "brain congestion;" and he suggested that it might be a sunstroke.

" Has he been much in the sun to-day?" asked the doctor.

" Somewhat," was the hesitating reply, and Burkhard shrank from his wife's accusing eyes.

The morning dawn found them all still around the sick-bed, where a burning fever was now raging, while the incoherent raving nearly broke Leonie's heart.

Little Toni came, and begged so earnestly to be permitted to see his friend, no one could refuse him. He sat in a corner, and, white as death, fixed his eyes on the invalid, who in his delirium cried out " Toni, Toni!" Toni came forward, and took the burning hand in his, but the sufferer did not know him. Wild fancies and cries of pain alternated, and then gave way to a state of semi-unconsciousness, until on the third day Baldo was dead.

Leonie threw herself on the little body, and would not let it out of her arms. She heard nothing, saw nothing, and the bystanders remained powerless before her wild grief.

Toni approached her, and, choked by sobs, said, " May I not kiss him ? "

The sound seemed to thaw the stream of tears which burst forth. She drew her darling's little friend towards her, and stroked his head fondly when he said, " Friedlein is cold."

It was four days before she could be induced to let the little corpse be buried.

Burkhard came into the room two or three times, but quickly went away again, for he could not bring himself to look on the dead.

Once again it was Toni who brought comfort to Leonie's poor, stricken heart. He brought some flowers, saying, " Now he has much more beautiful flowers in heaven, has he not ? "

She felt ashamed of the selfish sorrow
that would deprive her angel of heaven,
and, recovering something of her old
courage, gave directions for the funeral.

Over the grave she erected a simple
white cross with merely the word " Friedlein " engraved.

For many weeks the quiet of death
prevailed all over the estate. Leonie
could not bear the sight of children ;
even Toni she saw but seldom, and then
generally at Baldo's grave, for which they
both loved to care.

She continued to be the generous
helper of the poor, the conscientious
mistress of her house ; but every action
seemed actuated by a stern sense of duty,
particularly all relating to Burkhard, who
remained out of doors as much as possible.

She staid alone in the silent house ;
her lips set closer and closer, as if she

had forgotten how to speak ; and her
eyes over-spread with a far-off, dreamy
look, as though she herself were of the
dead.

The world went on.   Wilma had come
to ask her pardon if her thoughtlessness
had been the cause of Baldo's death.
Leonie could not see her, and Burkhard
had to receive her.

Wilma was so inconsolable in her self-
accusation that he said the boy had
always had a too excitable brain, and
had been too much forced in his studies,
so that the ride had probably at the worst
but accelerated the end.

Soon it was reported that Leonie
blamed herself so for having made
Baldo study too much, she was on the
eve of becoming crazy.

People looked at her askance, which
she interpreted as sympathy, and took a
sad pleasure in the belief that her darling was so universally mourned.

CHAPTER III.

WILMA.

The first time that Leonie again saw Wilma was on the occasion of a ride in the woods, which Burkhard had proposed. "It is such a beautiful day," he said. "We shall not have many more such; and then you will have the whole winter to imprison yourself, as seems to have become your delight of late." The closing part of the sentence was said with a certain tone of impatience.

"You are right," she replied. "But really, you appeared to have forgotten that I could ride: it did not occur to me that you had missed me."

She hastened to put on her riding-habit. He looked after her with a frown;

but when mounted, he could not but admire her dexterity in managing her horse, as if she had been constantly in the saddle. Her perfect fearlessness showed itself when she was on horseback.

It was late autumn ; the dry leaves rustled beneath the horses' hoofs, and the sun's rays shone through the bare branches, or few remaining golden leaves. Leonie rode a chestnut horse, whose glossy coat rivalled his mistress's own golden locks as they floated in the bright air. They halted at a spot which commanded a good view, and Burkhard pointed with his whip to the different objects of interest. She drew aside the veil which she had worn of late, and her eyes seemed to wander farther and farther. " Oh, yes ! " she cried suddenly, " that is the ride we took so often in our early married life ; and how you once teased me, Burkhard, just by those beeches! Do you remember?"

He made no reply, and a sigh escaped Leonie. He had joked with her on the probability of an heir ; and now both their thoughts were travelling back over the path of life, which in those days seemed so smooth, but which had had so many windings. They were so buried in silence that the sound of horses' feet and a call of recognition startled them ; and turning round, they perceived Wilma mounted on her black Arabian, and apparently embarrassed, as she said, " I had no idea, — it was so still! I beg a thousand pardons if I disturb you."

Burkhard had turned very red, and exhibited an awkwardness quite foreign to his usual cool self-possession.

Leonie answered in a friendly tone, " You do not disturb us in the least. Why should we not all enjoy the beauti-

ful day together? We were going to
Wildhof; and, if it be agreeable to you
to accompany us, it will give us a great
deal of pleasure."

Burkhard could not believe his ears.
What could Leonie mean? He had
never gone to Wildhof since the fatal
ride with Baldo. She, however, turned
her horse in that direction, and the
others exchanged glances in silence.
Did Leonie know that Wildhof was two
hours away?

Wilma had anticipated that their first
meeting would be at least stiff, and now
every thing had come about so simply.
Leonie was almost gay in manner, and
yet a troubled cloud hung over her
brow. After riding some time she suddenly turned around, and looked earnestly at her companions, who both turned
red. She became deathly pale, and
galloped on. Her eyes betrayed the

agitation of her soul; they were alternately brilliant and overcast, — not unlike the glowing rays of the sun and the dark shadows of the beéch-trees.

When the road became broader, she reined up, and let Wilma ride between her and her husband, saying, "The autumn air makes one hungry; at Wildhof we can get milk and particularly good black bread. The hostess is quite proud of it."

"You did not know, or had forgotten, how long a ride it was, Leonie," said Burkhard.

"Then I must indeed have a very short memory."

The answer sounded simple, but to Burkhard it was like a slap in the face. They tried in vain to hit on some indifferent subject, and lapsed into silence until Leonie said, "Here is the house. — Rademann, give the young lady something to eat. She wants to taste your bread. — Burkhard, will you do the honors? I want to catch the view over there, you know, the path by the oaks."

Without waiting for an answer, she set off on a gallop, and soon disappeared in the oak wood which still tenaciously kept its foliage.

"Will you dismount?" asked Burkhard, as he stood close to Wilma, and looked into her eyes.

"Oh, no!" she answered; but she seemed as though she could cry, and fall into his arms, her annoyance was so unbearable. She hated Leonie who tortured her, and she pitied more than ever the man who she thought deserved so much happiness in his marriage. Without doubt, she said to herself, Leonie worried him with her jealousy, and had undertaken this ride only just to see how they would act together. But she had seen nothing, absolutely nothing, and not a word had been spoken. If the ride home were only over!

All these thoughts passed through Wilma's brain while Burkhard handed her the bread and milk, and was answering the remarks of the host absently.

The contrast between the black bread and her white teeth, and the beautiful color in her cheeks, occupied his mind more than Leonie's conduct.

Leonie had reached the desired spot, which commanded the view of a somewhat ruined castle, situated on a wooded eminence at the foot of which a calm stream wound its way. She looked fixedly at it; her bosom rose and fell as the breeze waved her long veil about like a flag of distress. A tear trickled slowly down her cheek, and fell on her habit; she wiped it away with her handkerchief, and hastily dried her eyes as she heard the sound of the horses coming towards her, and busied herself with buttoning her gloves.

" The bread was very good," said Wilma. " But oh, how beautiful it is here! In all my wanderings I never chanced on this spot."

" It is homelike," assented Leonie.

" Homelike, — that I am not so sure of : ghostly, rather, and very mysterious."

" Leonie has a great fancy for this ruin of Altwehringen," said Burkhard. He and Wilma seemed very much excited, but Leonie did not appear to notice it as she remarked, —

" I think it would be lovely to live there."

" It depends on with whom," Wilma added laughingly.

" Alone, of course," continued Leonie, as she looked with wide-open eyes at the young girl.

"Alone!" exclaimed Wilma, with a shudder.

On their way home Leonie made her young companion talk incessantly ; and, as it was growing dark, she decided to accompany her as far as her father's house, saying, " They will be uneasy about you. You must excuse me for keeping you out so late."

" I never allow any one to be anxious on my account," was the pert reply ; but the blood flew to her cheeks, for she remembered the ride with Baldo. She was nervously excited on the way home, owing to the discomfort which Leonie's presence caused her. She breathed quickly as she went up-stairs to change her dress; and having laid her hat on the bed, she stood opposite the glass, looking at her dishevelled hair, as an elder brother came in with a hurried step, and asked, " What do you mean by this late ride ? "

" To amuse myself."

" But it does not amuse us ; and father
sends you word not to appear before
him this evening, but to consider how it
makes him feel to have you riding at this
hour with an admirer. Were I in your
place, I would be ashamed."

" Have you done?" inquired Wilma
with evident amusement. " Please to
understand that his wife took me with
them. With her have I ridden, and she
it was who took such a round, and begs
papa's pardon for bringing me home so
late. She feared you would be anxious."

" What can it mean?" said the young
man, puzzled. " It is perhaps her whim."

" That woman has no whims, and never
acts without a reason. What can it be ? "
This was the question which Burkhard
also was asking himself as he rode home
silently. He could not fathom his wife.
Arrived at home, she merely took off her

hat in order not to keep him waiting for
dinner. She looked very pale, and did
not utter a word until they had gone to
the drawing-room, and he had lighted
his cigar. Then she went to him, still
clad in her riding-habit, and said, —

" Burkhard, we shall separate."

He sprang to his feet, and said,
" Never ! "

She drew him gently back, and added,
" Do not say that, Burkhard. I know
you better than myself, because I love
you better than myself, notwithstanding
that I have failed to make you happy."

" I was not worthy of you," replied
her husband.

" No, no, do 'not say that. I have
always had the highest respect for you,
and ever will ; and if Wilma becomes
your wife"—

" But I never thought of marrying
her."

"Of course not while I am in the way. Nevertheless she has great attraction for you ; and I believe, I hope, she loves you." Leonie's voice faltered as she continued, —

"At all events, she would marry you if it were possible."

"O Leonie! How can you? Do you count for nothing all the years past? I cannot part from you. I cannot exist without you."

"You deceive yourself, Burkhard. For years you have made me conscious that I did not fill your heart. Then came another who for a little while contented you." Her lips trembled. "Now, since you have met Wilma, your heart belongs to her alone ; and it would be cowardly in me to usurp the place of another ; and she will bear you sons, and make you happy."

"Perhaps I have deserved these words

from you, Leonie, for not having made you happy. But I could not have believed that you would be jealous: I thought you above it."

. "Jealous! In the deepest examination of my heart I do not find the feeling, only the conviction that I am not sufficient for you, that each day you are disappointed in me, that you" —

"That I have lost my place in your heart, and cannot recover it."

"Perhaps you have not sought it."

. "Baldo found it, and filled it completely."

At this last remark of Burkhard's, Leonie's eyes fairly flamed as she said, "And you reproach me with this!"

"You say," continued Burkhard, "that I forget you; but you forgot me entirely for the child."

"You convince me, Burkhard, that I am not the right one for you. Let me go."

" Will you desert me, my only friend ? "

" I shall always be your friend, and I do not propose to go far away, — only to Altwehringen. There shall I reside, and be found when I am wanted."

" There — all alone ! " cried Burkhard, his eyes streaming in tears.

" Oh ! " replied Leonie, " I am better alone, — better alone." She thought, " My life is shattered and vain ; " but she merely said aloud, " You will mix with the world, and have a woman of the world for your wife. You cannot make me waver, Burkhard. I came to this conclusion many months since, but I could not summon courage to see you once with her. She is better than she is reputed, and she loves you."

Burkhard used all his eloquence to shake her purpose : who had ever made Leonie change her mind ? They talked during the greater part of the night, and

Burkhard often wept. For the moment it seemed to him that he hated Wilma, because she was tearing Leonie from him ; and his noble, unselfish wife never seemed more precious in his eyes. Yet she put it in the light of a duty before him that he should care for the perpetuation of his name ; and she concluded her arguments with the remark, "and I do not think that you need proof of how dear a child of yours can be to me."

· The following day Wilma was announced; and before Leonie had time to rise, the young girl stood before her, and, drawing a stool to her side, said, "I want to thank you for my lovely ride of yesterday. I was perfectly happy."

"Dear child," said Leonie, "are you not always bright and happy ?" A deep blush suffused Wilma's cheeks as she replied, "As much so as possible. I take pains to be so,"

" But were your heart content, it would require no pains."

" My heart! Do you, then, believe that I possess one? Hardly any one else gives me so much credit."

" For a long time I believed that your heart slumbered : now I know that it is awake, and lives, and suffers." Wilma looked startled ; but Leonie continued quietly, " Promise me that when your heart is satisfied, you will be a good wife, and never think that you can love too much."

" I never intend to marry."

" Do not say that, dear child. Heaven may take you at your word, and fulfil your wish."

" Heaven forbid ! "

" Heaven is often nearer than we think, and often it is closed before we know it. In either case must one have patience,"

At this moment Burkhard came in with
a hurried step, and seemed transfixed as
he perceived Wilma. She, however,
rose, and, going towards him, said, " I
came to return thanks for my nice ride.
My brother scolded me, and papa threat-
ened to imprison me in my room; but I
told them under whose protection I was,
then I could laugh at them, and, as
usual, I gained the victory."

These last words were like a burning
iron to Leonie; nevertheless, she said
smilingly, " You must always gain the
victory, dear child."

A few days later the whole neighborhood was excited by the report that
Burkhard and Leonie were seeking a
separation. All kinds of rumors were
rife, the most dramatic scenes pictured,
and Baldo's origin once more canvassed.
Altogether, there was a general excite-
ment, in which the parties most con-
cerned seemed the least interested.

Burkhard and Leonie were often seen going together to Altwehringen, which was being furnished with the belongings of the latter. She always looked kind and smiling, he sad and troubled.

Wilma alone suspected the true state of things, and she trembled to think of the final result. She either sat in deep, moody thought, or talked with nervous rapidity. One day her brother said to her, " I cannot rid myself of the idea that you are to blame for all this, and that you will now have it in your power to marry this man."

" Yes, that I will."

" Then I would not like to be in your place."

" But I will have him," replied Wilma slowly and deliberately.

CHAPTER IV.

THE snow lay deep on hill and dale,
and dark and gloomy frowned the ruined
castle which had once been the centre
of festivity. The lights were all extin-
guished, save in the corner tower,
whence shone a single lamp. At times
a shadow could be seen as if some one
leaned against the casement, then as
though a hand were raised to brush away
tears ; and again the falling snow veiled
all from outside observation.

Within, however, a homelike scene
presented itself. From the walls, well-
selected pictures looked down on luxuri-
ous furniture and rich carpets; a soft
divan, covered with a Persian rug, was

drawn up before the bright fire; the tables were covered with books, and in the corner stood a well-filled bookcase.

At a writing-table sat Leonie; it was the identical table at which she once read the warning letter. Again she read and re-read as before, but it was no letter now, but a newspaper; and, instead of stern decision, tears filled her eyes and streamed down her face unheeded.

She read the description of Burkhard's and Wilma's wedding, and prayed, " My God, graciously accept my offering. Let not my sorrow and sacrifice be vain. Grant him sons."

The newly married couple were glowingly described. Wilma was likened to an apparition from another world, captivatingly beautiful in the charming timidity which people discovered in her for the first time. The assembled company was distinguished and numerous; for

although many had shaken their heads,
and were shy of Wilma for months, few
felt they could brave the displeasure of
Burkhard, or dispense with his powerful
influence.

"Good God! grant that she may
love him," sobbed Leonie. "If she but
love him, I can welcome loneliness as a
punishment for not having pleased him,
and for my selfish grief for the child."

The poor, according to the account,
had not been forgotten; the bride had
ordered a Christmas festival for the children of the parish. Toni alone was
absent: he had gone as page with
Leonie, and had assisted her in making
preparations for the poorest children of
the village, to whom she had given
music, presents, and supper.

Of the village Christmas there was, of
course, no mention in the papers, nor
of how on Christmas morning Leonie's

pew in the old church was trimmed with evergreens, nor of how the venerable pastor had thanked God for having sent them a ministering angel. They told of the banquet which had been tendered to the newly married pair, and of their departure for the South.

The rich fur mantle of the bride was described ; but it was not told how, on being seated in the carriage, she threw herself into her husband's arms, exclaiming that she was *the happiest woman in the world,* nor how a momentary thought of Leonie had sent a fleeting shadow over Burkhard's brow, which filled Wilma with uneasiness and jealousy.

How peaceful the pure, cool snow-flakes seem in comparison to the odorous, luscious orange-blossoms which surround the bridal pair ! Leonie in imagination saw them in Sorrento, or perhaps in Genoa, on their way to the Riviera.

It seemed to her as if she remembered having once had youth and passion herself, which had been trodden down and frozen, — as if she had not had a cold nature! Even now when she thought of those orange-blossoms, and of Burkhard's blue eyes, her heart beat quickly; but she said to herself, " It was your own doing; you preferred to suffer rather than to make others suffer, now bear it! " She arose, put a log on the fire, and, drawing her spinning-wheel to her, took a book on her knee to read while she spun, as was her wont; but soon the wheel stood still, and the open book lay unheeded. Leonie gazed at the fire, which was sending up so many sparks, — useless sparks. Outside, flake upon flake, flake upon flake had fallen, until the whole world seemed wrapped in a bed of down, making Altwehringen look very peaceful.

The room door opened, and Toni appeared, rolling a small table towards his mistress, on which the tea and thin sandwiches looked appetizing; but Læonie's thoughts were so busy, she heeded not the singing. kettle or the sparkling logs. She had the fitful appetite of the lonely, and often forgot to eat, of which Toni was so aware that he was in the habit of coming in a second time, and announcing that tea was served, which made Leonie smile, and induced her to eat. But her imagination pictured cool ices eaten by the shores of the Mediterranean, and wafted the perfume of roses brought to her by Burkhard on their Southern trip.

Toni took the almost untouched meal away, and scolded the cook for not making something that his " dear lady could eat ; " at which she grew indignant that her cooking should be judged by the amount eaten or left. Leonie withdrew

to her bedroom, which was maiden-like
in its simplicity; and, as she let her long
hair fall around her, she looked like a
young girl.

In due time March, with its snow-
storms, passed away, and spring appeared, clothing the beeches with their
tender green, and the oaks with their
swelling buds, and filling the woods with
sweet songsters. One fine morning a
mounted messenger brought the following note: —

"With your permission I shall take a cup of
tea with you this evening.

" BURKHARD."

The note trembled in Leonie's hand,
and she wrote the hasty reply, " Heartily
welcome."

She would like to have written more,
but could not. What was there, indeed,
to write?

She laid aside her usual black dress, and put on the white cashmere which he used to admire. She looked like a bride as she hastened hither and thither, making every thing look bright, and drew the most comfortable armchair to the chimney-corner, and went out to look for the earliest snowballs.

A rider came quickly up the hill; and with a beating heart, but a cool exterior, she went to meet Burkhard, and, greeting him with the words, "God bless you, my friend," held out her hand, which he kissed. He seemed more aged than the eight months since she had seen him would warrant. Some silver threads, even, were visible in beard and hair, and the veins of his forehead swelled as she addressed him.

He offered her his arm, and led her towards the tower-room, saying, "I dared to come, for I could not bear to think that I was eternally banished from the roof which sheltered my guardian angel."

She answered, " I promised to be always your friend. Why, then, should you hesitate to come?"

"What a heavenly peace reigns here!" he sighed, as he looked around the room sadly.

Leonie's heart seemed to stand still at the possible thought that he was not happy, but she said gayly, —

" Is it not so? As if with an old friend shut in from the world. Now tell me of Italy and of Wilma, while I make the tea."

The word " Wilma" came so naturally from her lips, Burkhard looked at her in astonishment. She, however, was busy with her tea preparations, which helped to conceal the trembling of her hands.

"The journey was somewhat fatiguing," he said, as he dropped into his chair.

"And now I suppose you find much to occupy you on your return."

"Of course one cannot remain so long away from home without being punished, and now we have all those visits to receive. It is astonishing how much company we have at Grossheimbach, — almost too much."

"But that is all necessary with a large circle of acquaintance, and in order to extend your influence."

"Oh, my God! I have delegated my influence," laughed Burkhard.

"But why so?" asked Leonie, with an increased feeling of anxiety.

"Other hands now hold the sceptre like a May Queen, and I am not necessary."

"I would not entirely abdicate. That may be imprudent."

"Oh, I have become very imprudent. I do not think it worth the trouble to assert my authority. One must not be too imperative : you are thought much more agreeable and amiable if indifferent," Burkhard said cynically.

Every word was like a blow to Leonie. What had come over her proud Burkhard? And the worst was, he seemed unconscious of the change which had come over him. She tried to make him interested by asking if he had made many interesting acquaintances in Italy ; to which he answered languidly, "Not exactly interesting, at least they failed to interest me. I fear that I am very prejudiced, and have taken a narrow view of life."

Leonie remembered her travels with him in Italy, and how he had been such an intelligent cicerone, and had introduced her to so many who had left a deep impression. She said merely, —

"Of course a long residence in the country tends to decrease one's interest in society; its general topics pall on us for want of habit, and its aims seem of little consequence."

"After all, what is of consequence in life? Every thing seems hollow and trifling to me."

Leonie could not trust her ears. What had made a cynic of this jovial, happy man? Could it be possible that she had wrongly estimated his character? She continued to talk, but did not dare any further mention of Wilma, since he avoided the subject so persistently. Finally he stood up, and asked, —

"May I come sometimes?"

"Always," was the answer.

He kissed her hand, and was soon galloping down the hill; and Leonie's eyes followed him until he was out of sight. Then she sat long staring at the

spot where he had stood, and wondering if he were unhappy, or if it were
possible that the sacrifice she had made
was vain. No, no! she would not admit
the thought, or invoke such spectres.
She walked out on the balcony, from
which she gazed on the moon reflected
in the water of the moat, and on the
surrounding mountains rising in mighty
silence. The river at the foot of the hill
ran on and on, and the bats were dart-
ing in and out of the old chimney-stacks.
She watched the moon's lights and
shadows chase each other on the gray
walls, until such a restless homesickness
took possession of her, she wished for
wings. But alas, alas! wherefore wings?
They would only have to be clipped, and
forbidden to fly!

Summer brought numerous guests to
Altwehringen, the greater number out
of curiosity to see how the still young

woman contented herself in her owl's-
nest. They found her always cheerful;
generally surrounded by the poor and
sick, to whom she had grown the beloved
physician. The reputation of her numerous cures had become so extended that
she was left but little rest, the afflicted
from the farthest villages coming to soli-
cit her help. The pastor found her his
never-failing stand-by. They became the
closest friends; and, by their practical
assistance and advice, the poor soon
learned industry, and by intelligent
farming and thrift to materially increase
the value of their little holdings. She
established a sewing-school in which the
girls learned to make and mend their
clothes.

From early until late, Leonie was
busy; but whenever a certain horse's
tread was heard, every thing was laid
aside, and a careful toilet and hospitable
welcome made the dear rider happy.

Once he said, "It is inexplicable to me why there is now so much sympathy between us who at one time seemed to have nothing but misunderstanding."

"The simple explanation is, that for some time an unspoken reproach continually kept us apart."

"It was I," replied Burkhard, "who was at fault, and deserved the reproach."

"I am not so sure of that," said Leonie thoughtfully. "I had lost the path which led to your happiness, and could recover it only by a resolute step, hard to take."

"The path to my happiness, Leonie, is it recovered? and where is yours?"

"Mine? Oh, that does not matter. It was my right to accomplish your happiness, and, had it cost me my life, my friend" —

Burkhard interrupted her, and said with a deep sigh, "Leonie, I shall never forgive myself for having accepted such a sacrifice."

"Nonsense, nonsense!" replied the generous-hearted woman. "I am con·tent."

"Because I am not able to make you suffer any more," added Burkhard bit terly.

"Rather, because I am no longer a burden or an obstacle to your happiness, Burkhard."

"O Leonie, God alone knows which has been in fault!"

She felt her lips quiver; but she bit them, and said cheerfully, —

"I claim the right of having been a helpmate. Providence forbids criticism; and since I have assumed a little of that character, I insist that my dispensations be accepted without murmur."

"But," objected Burkhard, in a half sad tone, "Providence cannot suffer."

"And who says that I suffer?" asked Leonie.

He arose, took both her hands in one of his, and, stroking them gently, said, "Here I see the marks of martyrdom."

She drew her hands away, saying with a laugh, "Rather, the marks of years;" and then she commenced to speak of her flowers.

Some inquisitive friends happened in on such a scene; and, far from having the discretion to retire, they informed the whole neighborhood of how Burkhard had kissed her hands, and of how she called him her friend, and looked so youthful and dignified in his presence; also, what respect he showed her. Further, they told of how, on their boasting that they themselves had not set foot in Grossheimbach, she reproved them, saying, "Whoever loves me will not delay going there; how is it possible that a state of things brought about by myself could cause me pain ? "

Years passed. Burkhard began to grow gray, and yet no heir blessed his house. In his visits to Altwehringen he rarely spoke of Wilma. Others, however, were only too happy to bring news of her, telling how she was the social sun towards whom all turned ; how she daily grew more beautiful and also more extravagant; how her husband humored every whim, while she seemed so radiantly happy as to excite general envy.

The absence of an heir was much discussed ; for in that case the property would pass to distant relatives, and Wilma would be left very little. This state of things seemed to cost her no thought ; she was the leader of all gayety, while Burkhard often looked weary. He had lost much of his former influence by shirking duties and being indifferent to public questions in which he used to take so active a part.

Wilma's rooms were beautifully furnished, but showed no evidence of industry, with the exception of a small easel standing by the window, at which she painted flowers with a good deal of talent; and in this way she took part in many benevolent societies at whose bazaars her work was purchased at large prices by her many admirers.

Grossheimbach was much changed, more so than Altwehringen, whose new mistress's taste harmonized so completely with its characteristic quiet.

One autumn day, as Leonie was returning from some of her sick-calls, she noticed how the weather was changing. Thick mists arose from the river, and hung like white sheets on the castle walls. She had always had a great partiality for fogs; they threw weird shadows

on rooms and pictures, outlined the
shapes of the battlements, and, in clear-
ing away, left great tear-drops clinging
to the gray stones like dewdrops on
tropical plants.

The spiders were busily weaving their
webs and throwing filmy bridges from
stem to stem, and the moist atmosphere
hung diamonds from the tiny structures,
and the whole colony of workers, great
and small, toiled on. Leonie leant out
of the window to observe the industrious
creatures, lost in admiration at the perfect network which marked the track of
their spinning feet, when she was suddenly conscious of the approach of a
horse. In the next minute her room
door was thrown open, and Toni ushered
in Wilma, looking frightened and anxious. At a loss to imagine her business,
Leonie went to meet her visitor; but
before she could speak, Wilma knelt
before her, saying, —

"Forgive me! Oh, forgive me! I have done you a great wrong, and without your forgiveness Heaven will not bless me."

"Dear child," said Leonie softly, as she raised the young woman from the floor, "what has happened? Have I ever reproached you? Did I not always believe that you would make Burkhard happy? What, then, have I to forgive?"

"But I have not made him happy," sobbed Wilma. "He is so changed. At first I did not notice it, until I heard others say it. Now I am all anxiety, and yet I do not know what to do. He loves you much better than he does me, at which I do not wonder."

Leonie smiled, and, gently drawing her into the bedroom until they both stood before the mirror, said, "Only look."

Wilma saw herself in her brilliant

beauty and youth, standing beside a
woman in middle age, on whose brow
life's struggles had furrowed deep lines.
She turned to Leonie, and threw herself into her arms, saying passionately,
"Teach me a little of your magnanim-
ity of soul, only a little. Teach me how
to make him happy."

"You have not fulfilled your first
duty," said Leonie : "you have given him
no son."

"Too late, too late!" groaned Wilma.
"Has he unburthened his heart to you
and complained?"

"Burkhard? I think he would cut
out his tongue, rather than find fault
with you, dear child. It was entirely my
own suspicion, that perhaps his childlessness grieved him sometimes."

Leonie had poked the fire, and taken
her accustomed place at her spinning-
wheel; and Wilma knelt on the carpet

beside her. The sunlight through the
window, and the flames from the fire,
encircled both women with a halo of
light, as the one with earnest eyes
seemed to hang on the words which fell
from the lips of the other. The elder
knew human nature too well to weary
with useless preaching. In a sweet,
motherly manner she gave her young
companion truly practical advice; and the
latter, who had never known a mother's
care, cried, " Oh, why did I not come
here sooner? And when I think of how
I worried him with my petty jealousy all
these years! I always knew of his rides
here, and always made scenes before
and after; but he was as firm as a rock.
I might scold and pout; it was all useless when you were in question. Sometimes he observed complete silence; but
when he spoke he said, ' Wilma, on this
subject alone you cannot alter me; in

all things else you are my spoiled child.'
Then I concluded that he loved you
better than me.   Lately he became very
angry at one of these scenes, and said,
'Wilma, God will punish you for this.
Did you but know the saint of Altwehringen, you would kneel down before
her. You are not worthy of the sacrifice which she has made for you.'   I
never saw him so excited, and his anger
frightened me.   I was completely overcome, and determined to see you; and
now his words have proved true.   Your
countenance makes me feel so ashamed
of myself, that I must fall on my knees
before you.   Oh, how wretched I am!
How wretched I am!   How miserable
I have made him!   I cannot understand
my own blindness.   I was jealous from
the beginning, that I could not efface
you from his memory.   Forgive me, and
teach me how to win him back, and how

to atone for all those years that he has been so patient with all my moods. What a wasted life!"

Leonie felt each word as if it came from her own lips. In her egotism, Wilma did not realize what pain each confession of hers was inflicting on this lonely woman, whose strong will, however, controlled her aching heart, and who now acted with the judicious mildness of the best of confessors, as though she herself were entirely out of the question.

Thenceforward Wilma was even a more frequent visitor than Burkhard himself; until one day the latter came, looking younger than he had for a long time, and saying, "Wilma sent me to tell you that she does not feel equal to coming to-day," he took Leonie's hands in his, and kissed them, adding, "Leonie, you have made me happy."

CHAPTER V.

AT REST.

SUMMER had passed, and again autumn had come; and Leonie had sewed industriously the whole evening.

A white silk-lined basket filled with dainty garments stood before her; little shirts of finest linen, made with the skill of practised fingers; soft socks with blue ribbons. " Blue for a boy, pink for a girl," murmured Leonie to herself, as she smiled sweetly over her labor of love. Then she stood up, and raised a towel which covered a beautiful cradle made of blue silk and white lace, with embroidered pillows, and white quilted cashmere coverlet, — all her own work, for she wished that none other should make these preparations for the long-wished-for baby.

Wilma was a great sufferer ; and Burkhard was untiring in his attentions, reading aloud to her for hours tales of the simplest character, for all others tired her in her weak condition. He coaxed her appetite, and joked away her regrets that she had lost her good looks, and resorted to every expedient to while away the time that hung heavy upon her.

While Leonie stood before the prepared cradle, her thoughts wandered to Friedlein, until the long-dried-up tears found again their wonted courses. Time was effaced, and once more she lived that awful night when the first doubt of her husband entered her heart, and when Providence had sent her a son. She forgot that Baldo would have grown to manhood; and, thinking of " her baby," she wrung her hands, and threw herself

on her knees by her bedside praying,
" My God! Hast thou always been my
guide? Have I always obeyed thy laws,
or have I not rather followed my own
will? If my sacrifice has been pleasing
to thee, let my trial end, and take me to
thyself."

Overcome by weariness, she fell asleep
while still on her knees, and dreamed of
a spring storm, and of repeated knocking
at her door. She awoke, and smiled at
finding herself so, but was frightened by
an unmistakable summons to the door,
and hearing her maid, who appeared
ghastly pale, say, " A man on horseback
has just brought this letter."

Leonie opened it, and read, —

" For the love of God, come. Burkhard has
been taken suddenly ill, and is continually calling
for you.
                                    " WILMA."

She ordered the carriage, dressed

herself quickly, directed what was to be
sent after her, and stood at the castle-
gate before the horses were ready.

The lonely ride through the dark night
was made still longer by her impatience
to arrive. She now entered, for the first
time since the separation, the house of
which she had once been mistress, and
was met in the hall by a servant, of
whom she inquired all possible partic-
ulars.

The lips and hands of the faithful old
man trembled as he answered, " I don't
know what is the matter. The master
appears so strange. He has not been
well for some time, but laughed when
any one spoke of sending for the doctor,
until yesterday, when his chest was so
oppressed he could hardly breathe, and
he coughed continually."

He lighted her up-stairs, and without
hesitation she went to her former room.

As she entered, Wilma arose, and sobbed out, "They will not tell me the truth, but I know the trouble is in his lungs."

"Is that you, Leonie?" gasped the sick man, as he lay propped up with pillows, and begging for air.

Leonie hastened to his side; and he continued, holding her hand, "I knew you would come. I cannot die without you."

"But who speaks of dying?" she said in a re-assuring tone, while the great tears stood in her eyes. She rested on the bedstead, and drew Wilma forward, saying, "There, rest there. You must not excite yourself so."

Wilma hesitated until Burkhard said, "Do what she tells you, — do what she tells you. She will be a better pilot than I have been."

Notwithstanding the best of care, the sickness gained ground. Leonie understood this from the second day. The evening of the third day, Burkhard asked Wilma to leave him a little while; and when she had gone out of the room, he turned to Leonie, and said, " Be her pro-tector, and the guardian of my son, — and forgive, — I beg, forgive me my sin."

He opened wide his arms, and drew her to him, as if lent new strength. But a fresh fit of coughing came. Wilma was summoned, and she could scarcely restrain a cry of terror as she noticed the death-hue upon his cheek.

Leonie placed her in his arms; but he had no word for her, and his dying gaze was fastened on Leonie, who smiled on him as long as he could see. Then she gently closed his eyes, placed the faint-ing Wilma on a sofa in charge of the doctor and nurse, who gently bore her from the room of death.

The door closed, Leonie abandoned herself to unrestrained grief. Taking the beloved head in her arms, and covering it with kisses, she cried and sobbed, " Mine, mine ! " She rubbed the dear hands, as if to bring back the warmth, and pressed a handkerchief to her own lips to stifle the cries which would come. The long-repressed torrent of her love burst forth with a passionate force, now that he could not be aware of it. In that hour the crushing sorrow of a whole lifetime swept over her soul like a wild hurricane.

The pillow on which the dead man lay was wet with her tears, and his hands were warm with the warmth of her clasp, but his features lay cold as marble ; and at length she was completely exhausted by the violence of her grief. She reproached Heaven for not granting her prayer to let her die with him. But life still ran lustily in her veins, and Fate had yet work for her to do.

A knock was heard at the door; and, going hastily to open it, she met the doctor, who had come to tell the grave apprehensions which he entertained for Wilma. She went hastily to the latter's room, and there found her in bed surrounded by her relatives, whom Leonie now saw for the first time, and who naturally looked at her with mistrustful glances. Wilma threw her arms round her neck, crying like a helpless child, "Leonie, darling Leonie! My sister, my mother, stay with me, I beg!"

Leonie quickly perceived how necessary she was, and remained, showing the strength of manly firmness and the love of womanly tenderness, until her presence at Grossheimbach seemed as necessary as if she had never left it.

For six long weeks of suffering the

poor young widow seemed to barely exist, until, on Christmas Eve, the near approach of motherhood gave her new life. All night long Leonie held her in her arms, as though she would impart to her some of her own strength. As the morning broke, and the infant wail was heard, she cried joyously, " Wilma, your child lives."

" *She* lives," said the physician.

" A daughter?" inquired Leonie.

He nodded, and all were silent.

Wilma's lips became ashy ; she stretched out her arms, moved her head, so as to rest it on Leonie's bosom, moaned, " Good-night. I want to go to sleep," and — died.

Again some one knocks.

Eighteen years had passed. Spring was once more showering her radiance and sweetness and beauty over

Altwehringen. Leonie sat at the church
organ, with snow-white hair, and her
eyes raised to the bright young creature
who stood beside her, warbling joyously
Bach's Whitsuntide cantata.

"No, Mona, that is not just right.
Here you must sing lower."

"O mother! how can I sing low,
when my whole soul is bursting forth?
I cannot restrain my voice. — My faithful heart, sing! rejoice!"

The glorious anthem rang through
the church, and winning blue eyes that
so strongly resembled Burkhard shone
deep and true. Leonie smiled. If the
young throat delighted to pour forth
joy, the aged eyes loved to witness it.

"Have I tired you?" asked the young
girl, as she pressed the white head to
her breast. "O mother, do not say that
you are weary this glorious morning!"

"No, my child; but remember the

beautiful book which is awaiting us, and which we found it so hard to leave."

" Oh, Michael Angelo! grand Michael Angelo! Mother, does it not seem like being back again in Florence and Rome, when we read his life? How happy we are, mother dear!"

"Yes, my child, very happy." A saintly smile illuminated Leonie's countenance as she answered.

The two tall, slender figures left the church, and mounted the path leading to the castle, greeted reverently by all whom they passed.

" Toni," called the young girl to the corpulent liveried waiter, " the butterflies are out, the thrushes are nesting, and a sparrow flew over my head to-day."

" And Minka has pups," added Toni.

" No! How many? Are they pretty? Are they spotted? Are they fat? Is

Minka contented?" This volley of questions assailed Toni, before he could say, "But nine are entirely too many to leave with Minka."

"Oh, but Toni, you must not drown them, you must not drown them! I will tell you what we can do. We will get a goat, and make her lie down and suckle five of them."

Mona rushed to Leonie, and said, "Mother, can we not hire Ammi's goat for Minka's pups? We will pay her well, and she will be delighted. Do you consent?"

"But, Mona, what will Ammi's children do?"

"We shall send them cow's milk, mother. May we?"

Without waiting for an answer, she was soon on her way to the village; and a quarter of an hour later she returned with a child leading a goat, which, in a droll way, she introduced to Minka as her wet-nurse.

Later, Leonie sat at her spinning-wheel, Mona beside her with an open book on her knee, when the latter suddenly raised her head, and said, " Mother, must I marry my cousin at Grossheimbach ? "

Leonie stopped her work, and asked quickly, " Who said so ? "

" My cousin himself. He came close up to me with his stupid face ; and when I withdrew as far away as I could, he followed, and said, ' The most sensible thing we can do is to get married, little cousin.' I answered, ' Very well ; if you will remain at Grossheimbach, and leave me with mamma at Altwehringen, I think it is the most sensible thing.' Then he laughed one of his silly laughs, Ho-ho-ho! and I slipped by him, and, making him a courtesy, said, ' Good-by, Mr. Husband, always remain sensible,' and I ran away. You understand, mother, when I marry, it will not be because it is *sensible*, but because I *love*, and love him as much as I do you. Even then, how could I leave you, mother? I am the battlements round about you."

The young girl knelt before Leonie, and hid her brown curls in her lap.

The next morning, Mona was seated on the top of a high wall. A mandolin hung by a red ribbon from her neck, and while her fingers improvised a sweet air her little foot beat time. Then she sang an Italian pastoral, ending with a birdlike trill so long and clear it seemed as if her breath were inexhaustible.

She did not suspect that beneath her a traveller stood, and, by means of a field-glass, observed every movement of her countenance and throat as, clearly as the fluttering of a bird.

He had supposed himself in an abandoned vineyard, and that the old castle was uninhabited, and had just arranged his book to sketch, when the young singer attracted his attention. At first he was frightened at her dangerous position; then as song after song came floating on the air, he stood transfixed until a full low voice called, " Mona!"

" Yes, mother," sounded from above; and like a young chamois Mona leaped from stone to stone, using her hands to pull a straggling vine and wind it around her head, until she stood face to face with the stranger, who raised his hat, and said, " Young lady, can you tell me to whom this ruin belongs?"

" To my mother."

" Do you often visit the charming spot?"

" No, we live here."

The stranger stepped back, exclaiming, "Live here! I would not have supposed it possible. Only as a summer residence, no doubt?"

"We remain here also in winter, except when we go to Italy."

"In this lonely spot?"

"Oh, we are never lonely. In the first place, mother and I are always together; then we have the pastor, and the poor people, and all the animals."

The stranger laughed with such a musical laugh which lighted his eyes and countenance. Mona could not but be pleased as he said, —

"Then the nightingales must have been your singing teachers."

"Perhaps so when I was a child; but as I grew up my mother taught me, and I had a master in Italy."

"Were you there long?"

"Two years."

"What pleased you most there? I am positive I know."

" First the Moses, the Christ in the Vatican, then the Medici chapel in Florence. Shall I tell you what pleased me in Italy? Every thing."

" Mona!" again called a voice.

" May I continue to sketch?" asked the artist.

" Oh, certainly. I shall ask mamma."

" Many thanks. I shall take the liberty of paying my respects to your mother."

" Good-by, then," and the lithe figure disappeared. The stranger went directly to the pastor to inquire about the inhabitants of the castle, and, on hearing their history, begged to be presented to them.

As Mona came along the terrace, she seemed so thoughtful Leonie asked, —

" What is the matter, child?"

" I was thinking of Italy."

" Did those songs lead your thoughts there?"

" Yes, at first; then I met a stranger, I think a painter, who was speaking of it. He seemed so much astonished when I told him the castle belonged to my mother. You should have seen his face, and when he laughed it was in a minor key. He seemed so different from other people."

" Have you been long speaking with him ? "

" Oh, no ! you called me just then."

Leonie looked anxiously into the sweet face, and said, smiling, —

" It would be too bad if travellers should take it in their head to come rummaging in our old ruin."

" Mother, not if they were nice ! "

" With whom one could speak about Italy. Is it not so ? "

Mona laughed, and said, "And to whom one could sing in church."

" Perhaps he would not listen to us."

"Mother, no one with such a laugh could be unmusical, — trust me."

The day following this conversation, the pastor brought the young artist to the castle, and introduced him as "Graf Burkhard Liegenau."

Leonie could not hear the name pronounced without a deep impression, and a single look at her child showed how she was pleased with the visitor.

Love-making in Altwehringen, and a wedding in the little church suggests a romance of itself; and when such a being as Mona is in question, it needs not even such poetic surroundings.

"Mother, he has told me that he loves me. Do you know what that means? It is as if the sun shone on a little leaf, and made it a tree. Mother, do you understand?"

"Yes, child, I think I understand."

"Mother, if he ceased to love me, I would rather die."

" One is not always able to die, child."

" O mother, how could I live without love? Oh, no! you do not understand."

" Perhaps not, dear."

" And, mother, when he called me ' his all,' my heart leaped, and I trembled."

On the day of the wedding, Leonie said to the young bridegroom, " Promise me to be ever true to my child, to remember your vow; for, oh! you know not what it is to break a loving heart! "

Mona looked a very angel of beauty as the carriage, covered with a shower of rice and flowers, bore her and her husband away. Leonie went to her lonely room, and, falling before the chair where her own Burkhard had last sat, she prayed, " Good God, my last trust is fulfilled. Take me, I have waited so long! "

The strong woman's prayer was heard. For the first time she was unable to rise from her bed, and the pain in her heart increased so much that those around her determined to send for the young couple. For weeks and months she suffered uncomplainingly; and Mona showed her the love and tenderness of a devoted daughter, in which Burkhard united with the affection of a true son. He lifted her carefully, was always ready to read to her, and in every thing so vied with Mona in nursing that Leonie declared those were the happiest days of her life. Her bodily suffering was often almost unbearable; but, true to her nature, she used every effort to conceal it. To see her, her snow-white hair like a nimbus of glory around her spiritualized face, and to hear the precious words of love and sympathy for the young lives beside her, one would hardly believe they were witnessing the death-bed of a martyr.

One day as she sat with her hand in that of her son-in-law, listening to Mona's clear young voice, she said to him, "It grieves me deeply that I was obliged to recall you from your travels, and now have to keep you here from your own home;" to which he answered, "Dear mother, we thank God for every hour he allows us to be near you."

As Mona watched beside her one night, she said, "Mother, can I not call my child Leo, or Leonie? I pray that it may inherit your brave soul."

She did not understand the strange expression that came over her mother's face, for she was ignorant of the past. Leonie's eyes grew larger and larger as they retraced the thorny path of life, and the heart-strings seemed to tighten as the word "childless" came to her lips like a ghost that had dogged her every step in life. She smoothed her brow, smiled, and said, " Promise me, my child, that children will ever be a blessing to you, and that each new-comer will have the welcome of the first."

The aged pastor visited her often, and went away from each visit consoled and strengthened.

" I have wandered through the shadows of death," she would say, " but they have conducted me to heaven. Now all is clear. At first I murmured because I had to live; now I know that it was that I should live for Burkhard in his child. Now the darkness is dispelled, and I go forth into the light. No more doubt, no more trouble. Now I feel that God has accepted the sacrifice of my life, by the peace which he has granted me. Heaven must be very beautiful if man must suffer " —

An agony interrupted her speech, but she drew forth a small casket on which

was written " Remembrance," and gave
it to the pastor.

Turning to Toni, she said brokenly,
" Go — serve Mona, and her child —
tell them of — of — Friedlein." The
faithful Toni's tears prevented his answering.

As the sun was going down, a won-
derful light shone on her face as she
cried, " Mona! Do you not hear some
one knocking ? " Mona opened the door,
and said, " No, mother, no one knocks."
Again her countenance lighted, and she
murmured softly, " Some one is knocking. — Yes, I come. Burkhard! Friedlein! They are all there, and heaven is
open."

JOHN BROWN. By Hermann Von Holst, author of "Constitutional History of the United States," &c., together with an introduction and appendix by Frank P. Stearns, a poem by Mr. Wason, and a letter describing John Brown's grave. Illustrated. 16mo, gilt top. $1.50.

This book, the author of which is so well known by his "Constitutional History," and by his biography of John C. Calhoun, cannot fail to be of interest to all students of American history, who appreciate a calm, impartial criticism of a man and an episode which have been universally and powerfully discussed.

MARGARET; and THE SINGER'S STORY. By Effie Douglass Putnam. Daintily bound in white, stamped in gold and color, gilt edges. 16mo. $1.25.

A collection of charming poems, many of which are familiar through the medium of the magazines and newspaper press, with some more ambitious flights, amply fulfilling the promise of the shorter efforts. Tender and pastoral, breathing the simple atmosphere of the fields and woods.

AROUND THE GOLDEN DEEP. A Romance of the Sierras. By A. P. Reeder. 500 pages. 12mo. Cloth. $1.50.

A novel of incident and adventure, depicting with a strong hand the virile life of the mine that gives its name to the story, and contrasting it with the more refined touches of society in the larger cities; well written and interesting.

SIGNOR I. By Salvatore Farina. Translated by the Baroness Langnau. 12mo. Cloth. $1.25.

A dainty story by an Italian author, recalling in the unique handling of its incidents, and in the development of its plot, the delicate charm of "Marjorie Daw."

MIDNIGHT SUNBEAMS, OR BITS OF TRAVEL THROUGH THE LAND OF THE NORSEMAN. By Edwin Coolidge Kimball. On fine paper, foolscap 8vo, tastefully and strongly bound, with vignette. Cloth. $1.25.

Pronounced by Scandinavians to be accurate in its facts and descriptions, and of great interest to all who intend to travel in or have come from Norway or Sweden.

WOODNOTES IN THE GLOAMING. Poems and Translations by Mary Morgan. Square 16mo. Cloth, full gilt. $1.25.

A collection of poems and sonnets showing great talent, and valuable translations from Gautier, Heine, Uhland, Sully-Prudhomme, Gottschalk, Michael Angelo, and others. Also prose translations from the German, edited and prefaced by Max Müller.

Cupples and Hurd,   *Publishers, Booksellers, Library Agents,*   **BOSTON.**

Important New Books.